T0195574

Entries

Also by Wendell Berry

Fiction
The Discovery of Kentucky
Fidelity
The Memory of Old Jack
Nathan Coulter
A Place on Earth
Remembering
Watch with Me
The Wild Birds
A World Lost

Poetry
The Broken Ground
Clearing
Collected Poems: 1957–1982
The Country of Marriage
Farming: A Hand Book
Findings
Openings
A Part
Sabbaths
Sayings and Doings
Traveling at Home
The Wheel

Essays
Another Turn of the Crank
A Continuous Harmony
The Gift of Good Land
Harlan Hubbard: Life and Work
The Hidden Wound
Home Economics
Recollected Essays: 1965–1980
Sex, Economy, Freedom & Community
Standing by Words
The Unforeseen Wilderness
The Unsettling of America
What Are People For?

Entries

Wendell Berry

COUNTERPOINT

NEW YORK

First Counterpoint paperback edition 1997. Originally published 1994 by Pantheon Books.

Some poems were originally published in the following publications: "For the Explainers," *Ploughshares*, VII-2&3 • "A Marriage Song," *Ironwood 25* • "Voices Late at Night," "The Wild Rose," "Leaving," and "Thirty More Years," *Kentucky Poetry Review* • "A Difference," "The Record," and "Duality," *The Hudson Review* • "A Parting," *Blind Donkey* • "One of Us," *The American Voice* • "In a Motel Parking Lot, Thinking of Dr. Williams," *Chronicles* • "To My Mother," *Poetry* • "The Blue Robe," *Cow In The Road* • "The Venus of Botticelli," *Harvard Magazine* • "A Third Possibility," "A History," "Touch-Me-Not," and "Spring," *County Journal* • "On a Theme of Chaucer" and "Drouth," *Journal of Kentucky Studies* • "The Reassurer" and "Let Us Pledge," *The Amicus Journal* • "The Vacation," *Wilderness* • "The Three," *Sequoia* • "The Widower," *Explorations*

The poems in Part I were published as a chapbook by Confluence Press in Lewiston, Idaho.

Library of Congress Cataloging-in-Publication Data
Berry, Wendell, 1934–
    Entries / Wendell Berry. — 1st Counterpoint pbk. ed.
    I. Title.
    [PS3552.E75E58 1997]
    811'.54—dc21   97-7191
    ISBN 1–887178–37–6 (pbk. : alk. paper)

Book design by Fearn Cutler • Cover design by Amy Evans

Printed in the United States of America on acid-free paper that meets the American National Standards Institute Z39-48 Standard.

COUNTERPOINT

387 Park Avenue South
New York, NY 10016-8810.

Counterpoint is a Memper of
the Perseus Books Group.

10 9 8 7 6 5

✦ Contents

Some Differences

In memory: Harlan and Anna Hubbard

❧ For the Explainers

Spell the spiel of cause and effect,
Ride the long rail of fact after fact;
What curled the plume in the drake's tail
And put the white ring round his neck?

❧ A Marriage Song

In January cold, the year's short light,
We make new marriage here;
The day is clear, the ground is bridal white,
Songless the brittled air
As we come through the snow to praise
Our Mary in her day of days.

In time's short light, and less than light, we pray
That odds be thus made evens,
And earthly love in its uncertain way
Be reconciled with Heaven's.
Before the early dark, we praise
Our Mary in her day of days.

Now let her honest, honored bridegroom come,
All other choice foregone,
To make his vows and claim and take her home,
Their two lives made in one.
He comes now through the snow to praise
Our Mary in her day of days.

All preparation past, and rightly glad,
She makes her pledge for good
Against all possibility of bad,
Begins her womanhood,
And as she walks the snow, we praise
Our Mary in her day of days.

Now, as her parents, we must stand aside,
For what we owed we've paid her
In far from perfect truth and love—this bride
Is more than we have made her,
And so we come in snow to praise
Our Mary in her day of days.

January 10, 1981

❧ Voices Late at Night

Until I have appeased the itch
To be a millionaire,
Spare us, O Lord, relent and spare;
Don't end the world till it has made me rich.

It ends in poverty.

O Lord, until I come to fame
I pray Thee, keep the peace;
Allay all strife, let rancor cease
Until my book may earn its due acclaim.

It ends in strife, unknown.

Since I have promised wealth to all,
Bless our economy;
Preserve our incivility
And greed until the votes are cast this fall.

Unknown, it ends in ruin.

Favor the world, Lord, with Thy love;
Spare us for what we're not.
I fear Thy wrath, and Hell is hot;
Don't blow Thy trumpet until I improve.

Worlds blaze; the trumpet sounds.

O Lord, despite our right and wrong,
Let Thy daylight come down
Again on woods and field and town,
To be our daily bread and daily song.

It lives in bread and song.

✻ A Difference

Machines pass on the road, so heavy
that the leaves of the young beech,
spreading in stillness, shake.

But on the river, slow waves
roll under quick waves,
causing the reflections of the trees
to ripple and to sway.

❧ The Record

My old friend tells us how the country changed:
where the grist mill was on Cane Run,
now gone; where the peach orchard was,
gone too; where the Springport Road was, gone
beneath returning trees; how the creek ran three weeks
after a good rain, long ago, no more;
how when these hillsides first were plowed, the soil
was black and deep, no stones, and that was long ago;
where the wild turkeys roosted in the old days;
"You'd have to know this country mighty well
before I could tell you where."

And my young friend says: "Have him speak this
into a recorder. It is precious. It should be saved."
I know the panic of that wish to save
the vital knowledge of the old times, handed down,
for it is rising off the earth, fraying away
in the wind and the coming day.
As the machines come and the people go
the old names rise, chattering, and depart.

But knowledge of my own going into old time
tells me no. Because it must be saved,
do not tell it to a machine to save it.
That old man speaking you have heard
since your boyhood, since his prime, his voice
speaking out of lives long dead, their minds
speaking in his own, by winter fires, in fields and woods,
in barns while rain beat on the roofs
and wind shook the girders. Stay and listen
until he dies or you die, for death
is in this, and grief is in it. Live here
as one who knows these things. Stay, if you live;
listen and answer. Listen to the next one
like him, if there is to be one. Be
the next one like him, if you must;
stay and wait. Tell your children. Tell them
to tell their children. As you depart
toward the coming light, turn back
and speak, as the creek steps downward
over the rocks, saying the same changing thing
in the same place as it goes.

When the record is made, the unchanging
word carried to a safe place
in a time not here, the assemblage
of minds dead and living, the loved lineage
dispersed, silent, turned away, the dead
dead at last, it will be too late.

A Parting

From many hard workdays in the fields,
many passages through the woods,
many mornings on the river, lifting
hooked lines out of the dark,
from many nightfalls, many dawns,
on the ridgetops and the creek road,
as upright as a tree, as freely standing,
Arthur Rowanberry comes in his old age
into the care of doctors, into the prison
of technical mercy, disease
and hectic skill making their way
in his body, hungry invaders fighting
for claims in that dark homeland,
strangers touching him, calling his name,
and so he lies down at last
in a bare room far from home.
And we who know him come
from the places he knew us in, and stand
by his bed, and speak. He smiles
and greets us from another time.
We stand around him like a grove,
a moment's shelter, old neighborhood
remade in that alien place. But the time
we stand in is not his time.

He is off in the places of his life,
now only places in his mind,
doing what he did in them when they were
the world's places, and he the world's man:
cutting the winter wood, piling the brush,
fixing the fences, mending the roofs,
caring for the crops under the long sun,
loading up the wagon, heading home.

❧ One of Us

Must another poor body, brought
to its rest at last, be made the occasion
of yet another sermon? Have we nothing
to say of the dead that is not
a dull mortal lesson to the living,
our praise of Heaven blunted
by this craven blaming of the earth?
We must go with the body to the dark
grave, and there at the edge turn back
together—it is all that we can do—remembering
her as she is now in our minds
forever: how she gathered the chicks
into her apron before the storm, and tossed
the turkey hen over the fence,
so that the little ones followed,
peeping, out of the tall grass, safe
from the lurking snake; how she was one
of us, here with us, who now is gone.

❧ Thirty More Years

When I was a young man,
grown up at last, how large
I seemed to myself! I was a tree,
tall already, and what I had not
yet reached, I would yet grow
to reach. Now, thirty more years
added on, I have reached much
I did not expect, in a direction
unexpected. I am growing downward,
smaller, one among the grasses.

❧ The Wild Rose

Sometimes hidden from me
in daily custom and in trust,
so that I live by you unaware
as by the beating of my heart,

suddenly you flare in my sight,
a wild rose blooming at the edge
of thicket, grace and light
where yesterday was only shade,

and once more I am blessed, choosing
again what I chose before.

❧ Leaving

Parting from you, rising
into the air, I enter again
the absence we came together in.
My ways in house and field
and woods have reached an end,
dismembered of each other
and of me. And you remain
on the earth we knew, already changing
into the earth you know.
Fire-driven through the air,
I go alone, a part
of what, together, we became.

❧ The Blue Robe

How joyful to be together, alone
as when we first were joined
in our little house by the river
long ago, except that now we know

each other, as we did not then;
and now instead of two stories fumbling
to meet, we belong to one story
that the two, joining, made. And now

we touch each other with the tenderness
of mortals, who know themselves:
how joyful to feel the heart quake

at the sight of a grandmother,
old friend in the morning light,
beautiful in her blue robe!

❧ The Venus of Botticelli

I knew her when I saw her
in the vision of Botticelli, riding
shoreward out of the waves,
and afterward she was in my mind

as she had been before, but changed,
so that if I saw her here, near
nightfall, striding off the gleam
of the Kentucky River as it darkened

behind her, the willows touching
her with little touches laid
on breast and arm and thigh, I

would rise as after a thousand
years, as out of the dark grave,
alight, shaken, to remember her.

❧ A Third Possibility

I fired the brush pile by the creek
and leaping gargoyles of flame
fled over it, fed on it, roaring,
and made one flame that stood
tall in its own wind, snapping off
points of itself that raved and vanished.

The creek kept coming down, filling
above the rocks, folding
over them, its blank face dividing
in gargles and going on, mum
under the ice, for the day was cold,
the wind stinging as the flame stung.

Unable to live either life, I stood
between the two, and liked them both.

❧ In a Motel Parking Lot, Thinking of Dr. Williams

❧ I

The poem is important, but
not more than the people
whose survival it serves,

one of the necessities, so they may
speak what is true, and have
the patience for beauty: the weighted

grainfield, the shady street,
the well-laid stone and the changing tree
whose branches spread above.

For want of songs and stories
they have dug away the soil,
paved over what is left,

set up their perfunctory walls
in tribute to no god,
for the love of no man or woman,

so that the good that was here
cannot be called back
except by long waiting, by great

sorrows remembered and to come,
by invoking the understones
of the world, and the vivid air.

❧ II
The poem is important,
as the want of it
proves. It is the stewardship

of its own possibility,
the past remembering itself
in the presence of

the present, the power learned
and handed down to see
what is present

and what is not: the pavement
laid down and walked over
regardlessly—by exiles, here

only because they are passing.
Oh, remember the oaks that were
here, the leaves, purple and brown,

falling, the nuthatches walking
headfirst down the trunks,
crying "*onc! onc!*" in the brightness

as they are doing now
in the cemetery across the street
where the past and the dead

keep each other. To remember,
to hear and remember, is to stop
and walk on again

to a livelier, surer measure.
It is dangerous
to remember the past only

for its own sake, dangerous
to deliver a message
that you did not get.

❧ To My Mother

I was your rebellious son,
do you remember? Sometimes
I wonder if you do remember,
so complete has your forgiveness been.

So complete has your forgiveness been
I wonder sometimes if it did not
precede my wrong, and I erred,
safe found, within your love,

prepared ahead of me, the way home,
or my bed at night, so that almost
I should forgive you, who perhaps
foresaw the worst that I might do,

and forgave before I could act,
causing me to smile now, looking back,
to see how paltry was my worst,
compared to your forgiveness of it

already given. And this, then,
is the vision of that Heaven of which
we have heard, where those who love
each other have forgiven each other,

where, for that, the leaves are green,
the light a music in the air,
and all is unentangled,
and all is undismayed.

PART TWO

❧ On a Theme of Chaucer

I never have denied
What faith and scripture tell,
That Heaven's host is glad,
Or that there's pain in Hell.

But what I haven't tried
I'll not put up for sale.
No man has ever died
And lived to tell the tale.

❧ A History

Certain and elect, a man is going to a happy place,
and coming after him are his wife and his daughters,
his daughters' husbands, his sons and his sons' wives,
all the sons and daughters of his sons and daughters,
their husbands and wives, and all their neighbors,
    many households,
and the flocks and herds of each household, many
    hundreds,
their herdsmen and shepherds and their households,
all trusting the elect man and the happy place always
somewhere farther on, always beyond the last hills.
In the country that they are passing through
they drive away the local people for their sin,
that they are not welcomers of a higher destiny.
As the passers pass, paths are worn under their feet
and under the wheels of their wagons, heavily loaded;
it rains, and the paths that carry a nation
of people and a nation of beasts carry water also,
and the ruts deepen. The flocks and herds graze
the grass, they browse the trees and shrubs; the people
cut down the trees for bridge timbers, for firewood;
they kill and scare away the game. They set fires
behind them to discourage pursuit. Behind them,
the way would not support such another passage.

They pass. The days and the seasons come and go,
    quietly,
as if remembering and then forgetting the disturbance
that has passed. The grass restores itself, reaches out
with tiller and seed into the paths and covers them,
the shrubs and the trees grow again, the black
scars turn green, the animals and the birds
return. The local people drift back to their places
from the rocky valleys where they went for fear,
and make again their houses and little fields. This
    place,
that the great nation passed in its hundreds of hundreds,
becomes again the place that they were searching for.

✸ The Reassurer

A people in the throes of national prosperity, who
      breathe poisoned air, drink poisoned water, eat
      poisoned food,
who take poisoned medicines to heal them of the poisons
      that they breathe, drink, and eat,
such a people crave the further poison of official
      reassurance. It is not logical,
but it is understandable, perhaps, that they adore
      their President who tells them that all is well,
      all is better than ever.
The President reassures the farmer and his wife who
      have exhausted their farm to pay for it, and have
      exhausted themselves to pay for it,
and have not paid for it, and have gone bankrupt for
      the sake of the free market, foreign trade, and the
      prosperity of corporations;
he consoles the Navahos, who have been exiled from their
      place of exile, because the poor land contained
      something required for the national prosperity,
      after all;
he consoles the young woman dying of cancer caused by a
      substance used in the normal course of national
      prosperity to make red apples redder;
he consoles the couple in the Kentucky coalfields, who

sit watching TV in their mobile home on the mud of
the floor of a mined-out stripmine;
from his smile they understand that the fortunate have
a right to their fortunes, that the unfortunate have
a right to their misfortunes, and that these are
equal rights.
The President smiles with the disarming smile of a man
who has seen God, and found Him a true American,
not overbearingly smart.
The President reassures the Chairman of the Board of the
Humane Health for Profit Corporation of America,
who knows in his replaceable heart that health, if
it came, would bring financial ruin;
he reassures the Chairman of the Board of the Victory
and Honor for Profit Corporation of America, who
has been wakened in the night by a dream of the
calamity of peace.

❧ Let Us Pledge

Let us pledge allegiance to the flag
and to the national sacrifice areas
for which it stands, garbage dumps
and empty holes, sold out for a higher
spire on the rich church, the safety
of voyagers in golf carts, the better mood
of the stock market. Let us feast
today, though tomorrow we starve. Let us
gorge upon the body of the Lord, consuming
the earth for our greater joy in Heaven,
that fair Vacationland. Let us wander forever
in the labyrinths of our self-esteem.
Let us evolve forever toward the higher
consciousness of the machine.
The spool of our engine-driven fate
unwinds, our history now outspeeding
thought, and the heart is a beatable tool.

❧ The Vacation

Once there was a man who filmed his vacation.
He went flying down the river in his boat
with his video camera to his eye, making
a moving picture of the moving river
upon which his sleek boat moved swiftly
toward the end of his vacation. He showed
his vacation to his camera, which pictured it,
preserving it forever: the river, the trees,
the sky, the light, the bow of his rushing boat
behind which he stood with his camera
preserving his vacation even as he was having it
so that after he had had it he would still
have it. It would be there. With a flick
of a switch, there it would be. But he
would not be in it. He would never be in it.

✤ A Lover's Song

When I was young and lately wed
And every fissionable head
Of this super power or that
Prepared the ultimate combat,
Gambling against eternity
To earn a timely victory
And end all time to win a day,
"Tomorrow let it end," I'd pray,
"If it must end, but not tonight."
And they were wrong and I was right;
It's love that keeps the world alive
Beyond hate's genius to contrive.

❧ Anglo-Saxon Protestant Heterosexual Men

Come, dear brothers,
let us cheerfully acknowledge
that we are the last hope of the world,
for we have no excuses,
nobody to blame but ourselves.
Who is going to sit at our feet
and listen while we bewail
our historical sufferings? Who
will ever believe that we also
have wept in the night
with repressed longing to become
our real selves? Who will
stand forth and proclaim
that we have virtues and talents
peculiar to our category? Nobody,
and that is good. For here we are
at last with our real selves
in the real world. Therefore,
let us quiet our hearts, my brothers,
and settle down for a change
to picking up after ourselves
and a few centuries of honest work.

⚓ Madness

In this age of nearly perfect
madness, that has politicized
everything but politics, favored
minorities and women will be
driven mad by the suspicion,
whenever they are rewarded,
that they have been rewarded
beyond their merits by political
sentiment replacing judgment.
And Anglo-Saxon Protestant
heterosexual men will be maddened
by the suspicion that, if only
uncorrupted judgment prevailed,
they would be found more deserving
than they have yet been found to be,
and perhaps more than in fact
they are. This madness comes
when the lineages of faith
and craft are severed, and the truth
of anything cannot be known
because anything supposable
can be endlessly supposed.

❧ Air

This man, proud and young,
turns homeward in the dark
heaven, free of his burden
of death by fire, of life in fear
of death by fire, in the city
now burning far below.

This is a young man, proud;
he sways upon the tall stalk
of pride, alone, in control of the
explosion by which he lives, one
of the children we have taught
to be amused by horror.

This is a proud man, young
in the work of death. Ahead of him
wait those made rich by fire.
Behind him, another child
is burning; a divine man
is hanging from a tree.

Enemies

If you are not to become a monster,
you must care what they think.
If you care what they think,

how will you not hate them,
and so become a monster
of the opposite kind? From where then

is love to come—love for your enemy
that is the way of liberty?
From forgiveness. Forgiven, they go

free of you, and you of them;
they are to you as sunlight
on a green branch. You must not

think of them again, except
as monsters like yourself,
pitiable because unforgiving.

The Mad Farmer, Flying the Flag of Rough Branch, Secedes from the Union

From the union of power and money,
from the union of power and secrecy,
from the union of government and science,
from the union of government and art,
from the union of science and money,
from the union of ambition and ignorance,
from the union of genius and war,
from the union of outer space and inner vacuity,
the Mad Farmer walks quietly away.

There is only one of him, but he goes.
He returns to the small country he calls home,
his own nation small enough to walk across.
He goes shadowy into the local woods,
and brightly into the local meadows and croplands.
He goes to the care of neighbors,
he goes into the care of neighbors.
He goes to the potluck supper, a dish
from each house for the hunger of every house.
He goes into the quiet of early mornings
of days when he is not going anywhere.

Calling his neighbors together into the sanctity
of their lives separate and together
in the one life of their commonwealth and home,
in their own nation small enough for a story
or song to travel across in an hour, he cries:

Come all ye conservatives and liberals
who want to conserve the good things and be free,
come away from the merchants of big answers,
whose hands are metalled with power;
from the union of anywhere and everywhere
by the purchase of everything from everybody at the lowest p
and the sale of anything to anybody at the highest price;
from the union of work and debt, work and despair;
from the wage-slavery of the helplessly well-employed.

From the union of self-gratification and self-annihilation,
secede into care for one another
and for the good gifts of Heaven and Earth.

Come into the life of the body, the one body
granted to you in all the history of time.
Come into the body's economy, its daily work,
and its replenishment at mealtimes and at night.
Come into the body's thanksgiving, when it knows
and acknowledges itself a living soul.
Come into the dance of the community, joined
in a circle, hand in hand, the dance of the eternal
love of women and men for one another
and of neighbors and friends for one another.

Always disappearing, always returning,
calling his neighbors to return, to think again
of the care of flocks and herds, of gardens
and fields, of woodlots and forests and the uncut groves,
calling them separately and together, calling and calling,
he goes forever toward the long restful evening
and the croak of the night heron over the river at dark.

◄ PART THREE ►

❧ Even in Darkness

Even in darkness, love
shows the circumference
of the world, lightning
quivering on horizons
in the summer night.

✶ Duality

*So God created man in his
own image, in the image of God
created he him; male and female
created he them.*

✶ I

To love is to suffer—did I
know this when first
I asked you for your love?
I did not. And yet until
I knew, I could not know what
I asked, or gave. I gave
a suffering that I took: yours
and mine, mine when yours;
and yours I have feared most.

✶ II

What can bring us past
this knowledge, so that you
will never wish our life
undone? For if ever you
wish it so, then I must wish
so too, and lovers yet unborn,
whom we are reaching toward
with love, will turn to this
page, and find it blank.

III

I have feared to be unknown
and to offend—I must speak,
then, against the dread
of speech. What if, hearing,
you have no reply, and mind's
despair annul the body's hope?
Life in time may justify
any conclusion, whenever
our will is to conclude.

IV

Look at me now. Now,
after all the years, look at me
who have no beauty apart
from what we two have made
and been. Look at me
with the look that anger
and pain have taught you,
the gaze in which nothing
is guarded, nothing withheld.

❧ V

You look at me, you give
a light, which I bear and return,
and we are held, and all
our time is held, in this
touching look—this touch
that, pressed against the touch
returning in the dark,
is almost sight. We burn
and see by our own light.

❧ VI

Eyes looking into eyes looking
into eyes, touches that see
in the dark, remember Paradise,
our true home. God's image
recalls us to Itself. We move
with motion not our own,
light upon light, day and
night, sway as two trees
in the same wind sway.

❧ VII

Let us come to no conclusion,
but let our bodies burn
in time's timelessness. Heaven
and earth give us to this night
in which we tell each other of
a Kingdom yet to come, saying
its secret, its silent names.
We become fleshed words, one
another's uttered joy.

❧ VIII

Joined in our mortal time,
we come to the resurrection
of words; they rise up
in our mouths, set free
of taints, errors, and bad luck.
In their new clarities
the leaf brightens, the air
clears, the syllables of water are
clear in the dark air as stars.

IX

We come, unsighted, in the dark,
to the great feast of lovers
where nothing is withheld.
That we are there we know
by touch, by inner sight.
They all are here, who by
their giving take, by taking
give, who by their living
love, and by loving live.

☙ The Three

A woman wholly given in love is held
by a dying man and an immortal one.
The man dying knows himself departing
from her, leaving her in the arms
of the man who will live, cherishing her,
given to him as she is forever.

❧ Touch-Me-Not

There is a flower called touch-me-not,
which means, of course, touch me,
for it depends upon touch for propagation,
as humans do. The blossom may be
two tones of orange, the darker exquisitely
freckling the lighter, or a clear lovely
yellow, an elegant aperture, inviting entry
by winged emissaries of imagination
actuated by love. The seed pods are made
of coil springs laid straight in the pod's
shape; ripe, the seeds are restrained in
suspension of tension. Touched, they fly.

✶ To Hayden Carruth

Dear Hayden, when I read your book I was aching
in head, back, heart, and mind, and aching
with your aches added to my own, and yet for joy
I read on without stopping, made eager
by your true mastery, wit, sorrow, and joy,
each made true by the others. My reading done,
I swear I am feeling better. Here in Port Royal
I take off my hat to you up there in Munnsville
in your great dignity of being necessary. I swear
it appears to me you're one of the rare fellows
who may finally amount to something. What shall
I say? I greet you at the beginning of a great career?
No. I greet you at the beginning, for we are
either beginning or we are dead. And let us have
no careers, lest one day we be found dead in them.
I greet you at the beginning that you have made
authentically in your art, again and again.

❧ Drouth

All day the crops burn in the cloudless air,
Drouth lengthening against belief. At night
The husbands and the wives lie side by side,
Awake, the ache of panic in their bones,
Their purposes betrayed by purposes
Unknown, whose mystery is the dark in which
They wait and grieve. All may be lost, and then
What will they do? When money is required
Of them, and they have none, where will they go?

Many will go in blame against the world,
Hating it for their pain, and they will go
Alone across the dry, bright, lifeless days,
And thus alone into the dark. Others
In grief and loss will see more certainly
What they have loved, and will belong to it
And to each other as in happiness
They never did—hearing, though the whole world
Go dry, the hidden raincrow of their hope.

❧ Noguchi Fountain

Sits level,
fills silently,
overflows,
makes music.

❧ Spring

A shower like a little song
Overtook him going home,
Wet his shoulders, and went on.

❧ Two Questions

If you provided a marriage feast
and the thankless guests crowded
at the table, gobbling the food
without tasting it, and shoving
one another away, so that some ate
too much and some ate nothing,
would you not be offended?

Or if, seated at your bountiful table,
your guests picked and finicked
over the food, eating only a little,
refusing the wine and the dessert,
claiming that to fill their bellies
and rejoice would impair their souls,
would you not be offended?

❧ Imagination

A young man's love is bitter love
For what he must forego,
For what he ignorantly would have,
Desires but does not know.

The years, the years will teach him joys
That are more bitter still;
What in his having he forgoes
He has imagined well.

❧ The Widower

After she died there came a day
In which he walked from room to room
And found in all the house no trace
Of her perfume. And then nothing
Reflected anything there, not mirror
By day, nor window after dark.

❧ Devon

Stone churches, seeking Heaven's face,
Rise from the ground and into grace.

In hedgerow and in stone farmstead
Earth shelters lives that it has fed.

Here lie the builders, rest their bones,
Their days subsided from these stones.

❧ For an Absence

When I cannot be with you
I will send my love (so much
is allowed to human lovers)
to watch over you in the dark—
a winged small presence
who never sleeps, however long
the night. Perhaps it cannot
protect or help, I do not know,
but it watches always, and so
you will sleep within my love
within the room within the dark.
And when, restless, you wake
and see the room palely lit
by that watching, you will think,
"It is only dawn," and go
quiet to sleep again.

❧ The Storm

We lay in our bed as in a tomb
awakened by thunder to the dark
in which our house was one with night,
and then light came as if the black
roof of the world had cracked open,
as if the night of all time had broken,
and out our window we glimpsed the world
birthwet and shining, as even
the sun at noon had never made it shine.

PART FOUR

When thou wast young, thou girdest thyself, and
walkedst whither thou wouldest: but when thou
shalt be old, thou shalt stretch forth thy hands,
and another shall gird thee, and carry thee whither
thou wouldest not.

John 21:18

In Extremis: *Poems about My Father*

I was at home alone. He came
to fight, as I had known he would.
The war in Vietnam was on;
I'd spoken out, opposing it—
and so, I thought, embarrassed him.

Not because he loved the war.
He feared for me, or for himself
in me. Fear angered him. He was
my enemy; his mind was made
up like a fist. He sat erect
on the chair's edge as on a horse,
would not take off his coat.
That was his way. My house was not
a house in which he would consent
to make himself at home that day.

The argument was hard and hot.
Tempered alike, we each knew where
the other's hide was tenderest.
We went past reason and past sense
by way of any eloquence
that hurt. He leaned. I saw the brown

spot in the blue of his right eye.
Forefinger hooking through the air,
he said I had been led astray,
beguiled, by he knew who, by God!

And was I then to be his boy
forever? Or his equal? Or
his foe? His equal and his foe?
By grace (I think it must have been
by grace) I told him what I knew:

"Do you know who has been, by God,
the truest teacher in my life
from the beginning until now?"

"*Who*, by God?"

"*You*, by God!"

He wept and said, "By God, I'm proud."

II

He was, in his strength, the most feeling
and the most demanding man
I have ever known. I knew at first
only the difficulty of his demand,
but now I know the fear in it.
He has been afraid always of the loss
of precious things. We live in time
as in hard rain, and have no shelter,
half hopeless in anxiety for the young,
half helpless in compassion for the old.
The generations fail and we forget
what we were, and are. The earth,
even, is flowing away. And where
is the stay against indifference?
I know his fear now by my own.
Precious things are being lost.

My grandfather, in the lost tongue
of his kind and time, called drawers
"draws." My father pronounced the word
that way himself from time to time
in commemoration. And now another
time had come. I diapered him
like a child and helped him go
with short slow steps to bed. Meaning
to invoke his old remembrance
to cheer him, I said, "Don't lose
your draws." "We miss him, don't we?"
he said. "Yes," I said. "Yes," he said.

☙ IV

Sometimes we do not know what time he's in
Or if he is in time. The dead live in his mind.
They wait beyond his sight, made radiant by his long
Unchanging love, as by the mercy and the grace
Of God. At night I help him to lie down upon
That verge we reach by generation and by day.
He says that, though we sleep, we love eternally.

✿ V

He dreamed there was a storm
And all was overturned.
In his great need he called
His mother and his father
To help him, and one he'd known
But did not know found him
On the dark stair, led him
Back to his bed. Next day,
The dream still near, he said,
In longing of this world
That in the next is joy,
"If I could have found Papa,
I'd have been so comforted."

VI

I imagine him as he must appear
to his father and mother now,
if from the world of the dead they see
him as he now is—an old man
sliding his feet along the floor
in little childish steps. I imagine
that they call him "child," and pity
him, and love him as they did,
for they are senior to him still,
having gone through the dark door,
and learned the hard things and the good
that only the dead can know.
And I imagine that they know also
the greater good, that we long for
but cannot know, that knows
of all our sorrow, and rejoices still.

VII

Sometimes in sleeping he forgets
That he is old and, waking up,
Intends to go out in the world
To work, just as he did before—
Only to find that his body now
No longer answers to his will,
And his mind too is changed but not
By him. And then he rages in
His grief, and will not be consoled.
He cannot be consoled by us,
More mortal in our fewer years,
Who have not reached the limit he
Has come to, when immortal love
In flesh, denying time, will look
At what is lost, and grief fulfill
The budget of desire. Sometimes,
At home, he longs to be at home.

❧ VIII

And sometimes he fulfills
What must have been the worst
Of all his fears: to be
An old man, fierce and foul,
Outraged and unforgiving,
One man alone, mere fact
Beyond the reach of love.
For fear this is his fate,
And mine if it is his,
I struggle with him. Thus
We ardently debate
The truth of fantasy
Empowered by wrath—the facts
He says are lies, the lies
He says are facts—his
Eyes in their conviction hard
To meet, hard to avoid.
We go into a place
Of ruin, where light obscures,
The right place for us now
In our mad argument,
Exchanging foolish fire
In reasoned eloquence,
And winning no success.
We still are as we were,
And yet we do not fail,
For thus estranged we both
Oppose his loneliness.

IX

The dead come near him in his sleep
And, waking, he calls out to them
To help him in his helplessness.

And though they in their distance keep
Silent, and give no help to him.
And do not answer his distress,

I hear him calling in my sleep
Among the living in the dim
House, where he calls in loneliness.

I go to help him in the deep
Night, waked and walking in whose time?
I am the brother called in darkness.

X

We watch the TV show,
Smooth faces and smooth talk
Made for everywhere,
Thus alien everywhere.
In deference to old age
And time, we sit down for
What no one can stand up for.
I wish him out of it,
That man-made other world.
I wish undone his absence
In body and in thought
From open countryside,
Our local air and light.
To honor him aright
I call him back to mind,
Remember him again
When he was my age now,
And straighter-backed than I,
Still hungry for the world.
His mind was then an act
Accomplished soon as thought,
Though now his body serves
Unwillingly at best
His mind's unresting will.
I summon him away
From time and heaviness.
I see him as he was.

The light is low and red upon the fields,
The mists are rising in the long hollow,
The shadows have stretched out, and he comes walking
In deep bluegrass that silences his steps.
Elated and upright, he walks beneath
The walnut trees around the spring. His work
Is done, the office shut and still, his chair
Empty. And now at his long shadow's foot,
He comes to salt the ewe flock, and to hear
The meadowlarks sing in the evening quiet.
He calls his sheep, who know his voice and come,
Crowding up to him as the light departs
And earth's great shadow gathers them in. White
In darkening air, their fleeces glow as he
Puts down the salt, a handful at a place,
Along the path. At last, the bucket empty,
He stands, watching the sheep, the deepening sky,
The few small stars already pointing out.

Now may he come to that good rest again.

✻ XII

What did I learn from him?
He taught the difference
Between good work and sham,
Between nonsense and sense.

He taught me sentences,
Outspoken fact for fact,
In swift coherences
Discriminate and exact.

He served with mind and hand
What we were hoping for:
The small house on the land,
The shade tree by the door,

Garden, smokehouse, and cellar,
Granary, crib, and loft
Abounding, and no year
Lived at the next year's cost.

He kept in mind, alive,
The idea of the dead:
"A steer should graze and thrive
Wherever he lowers his head."

He said his father's saying.
We were standing on the hill
To watch the cattle grazing
As the gray evening fell.

"Look. See that this is good,
And then you won't forget."
I saw it as he said,
And I have not forgot.

❧ Epitaph

Having lived long in time,
he lives now in timelessness
without sorrow, made perfect
by our never finished love,
by our compassion and forgiveness,
and by his happiness in receiving
these gifts we give. Here in time
we are added to one another forever.

❧ Come Forth

I dreamed of my father when he was old.
We went to see some horses in a field;
they were sorrels, as red almost as blood,
the light gold on their shoulders and haunches.
Though they came to us, all a-tremble
with curiosity and snorty with caution,
they had never known bridle or harness.
My father walked among them, admiring,
for he was a knower of horses, and these were fine.

He leaned on a cane and dragged his feet
along the ground in hurried little steps
so that I called to him to take care, take care,
as the horses stamped and frolicked around him.
But while I warned, he seized the mane
of the nearest one. "It'll be all right,"
he said, and then from his broken stance
he leapt astride, and sat lithe and straight
and strong in the sun's unshadowed excellence.

A native Kentuckian, Wendell Berry lived and taught in New York and California before returning permanently to the Kentucky River region. For the last three decades he has lived and farmed with his family on 125 acres in Henry County. He is a past fellow of both the Guggenheim Foundation and the Rockefeller Foundation, and is a former Stegner Fellow at Stanford University. He has received, among other awards, the Victory of Spirit Ethics Award in 1992 from the Louisville Community Foundation and the University of Louisville, and the Lannan Foundation Award for Nonfiction in 1989.

Author of more than two dozen books of fiction, poetry, and essays, Wendell Berry currently lives and writes on his farm in Kentucky and teaches at the University of Kentucky.

Printed in the United States
by Baker & Taylor Publisher Services